# Selected Poems

Terence Watson

**Coventry Umbrella Club**

TAKAHE PUBLISHING LTD.
2015

First published in 2015 by

Takahe Publishing Ltd.
77 Earlsdon Street
Coventry CV5 6EL
www.takahepublishing.co.uk


Published with the permission of the executors for Terence Watson
This edition: Copyright © Coventry Umbrella Club, 2015

ISBN 978-1-908837-02-8

# Terence Watson

Photographed by Ann Hill (née Collins), a life-long friend

# EDITOR'S NOTE

Terence Charles Watson was born in 1920. He was educated at the Stationers' Company School in London and studied at Magdalen College Oxford where he read English under the tutorial guidance of C S Lewis. His studies were interrupted by service in the RAF in the Second World War and he finally graduated in 1947.

He taught for five years at Cottesmore School and came to Coventry in 1955 to take up a post at King Henry VIII School. Soon after, he joined the Umbrella Club which had recently been established to foster participation in all the arts for Coventry citizens. Through his involvement in the Umbrella Club Terry very quickly showed his commitment to all the arts even those in which he was not expert of which there were few! During those astonishing ten years at the Umbrella Club he showed his skills as literary editor, poet, theatre director, painter and exhibition curator and promoter as well as heading up the Umbrella Club organisation. Above all, he was passionate about encouraging artistic creativity in others, especially those who seemed to lack confidence in their own potential.

In later years, he taught creative writing at Tile Hill College. Still later, in his seventies, he became interested in yoga and practised to the degree that he qualified as a teacher of yoga (Sironami Tejas) in Florida, USA. He was also proud to be made a Freeman of the City of London and a member of the Worshipful Company of Stationers and Newspaper Makers.

It was Terry's wish that his poems should be published. The Coventry Umbrella Club is proud to make his wish come true with part of his bequest. This collection is divided into four sections. The first three are a miscellany of poetry with many moods (Living, Loving, Laughing) mostly written after 1947. The final section (Terry's War) contains the poems written while Terry was on active service.

I have edited the poems with as little alteration as possible. Terry showed great enthusiasm and skill in reading aloud both his own and other people's poetry. I have added a few punctuation marks to facilitate this. There are a few poems that are presented in the way in which they were written with neither punctuation nor capital letters.

Bob Wright

3 September 2015

# Living

# LIVING

# A Lovely Bunch

This is how I was taken in

By a bunch of flowers.

Saw this bunch of flowers in a friend's house

In the corner of a room in a black vase.

A tight bunch of michaelmas daisies

And some roses.

Ordinary all - pink, common or garden roses

And two or three fancy heads

Orange and white and pink and white

Lovely.

The stems of the michaelmas daisies

Were about one size

Each with a frizz of purple petals

Around a yellow - speckled centre.

There were also some neat little buds among the roses.

The fancy roses also had colours nicely graduated

From edge to heart of the curling petals.

Fresh

Clean

Perfect

Plastic of course.

The lot.

Too perfect for natural.

No damaged or dying heads for instance.

Colours with the vividness of synthetic dyes.

Out of season with each other.

Cleverly made

But with that hard, indestructible look.

Quite in character with the people of course.

Brash.

No taste.

What kind of satisfaction did they get

From such a piece of cheap stage dressing?

I wondered what the textures felt like.

They say these days they make them

With an almost natural feel.

I put out my hand and touched a rose petal

Silky soft.

Felt round the flower head

A petal detached and fell.

Real.

Real flowers.

The whole bunch.

Real flowers in real water.

Yes.

A disturbing experience.

Unnerving somehow.

*undated*

# In McDonald's

She pointed at the squares of coloured glass

Among the electric lights

In McDonald's fast food restaurant.

'God lives there', she said.

I said, 'Up there?  You really mean...'

'Well, not quite.' she said.

It must have been a memory of stained glass

Somewhere.  At an east end.  Behind a reredos.

But her first formulation packed a punch.

If God lives anywhere...  If God lives...

Where better than behind the glass,

Among the lights, above the table,

In McDonald's Restaurant,

Where everybody goes.

*July 1991*

# Morning Flight

Four twin jets in a clear sky
Chalk sharp lines in the clear air.
Eight streaks rear, and falling
Criss - cross above the rising sun.  Eight
Thin tips bore into the far haze.

Meeting someone else
Is crossing a line in the sky.
Two separate beginnings
Are together once.  Beyond -
Lines divide.  Memory remains,
Streaks in the sky from the planes.

Lazily the thin tips broaden into wide
Grey bands draped through pale blue.  Tips
Are lost in the east.  The criss - cross blurs.
All dim traces fade.  The sky curves sheer
Above long clouds rimming the incendiary horizon.

*1951*

## On Reading Bill Tait's 'A Day Between The Weathers'

These verses generate within my mind

An image of the man, his movements, his way

Of speech, manner, expression, things he'd say,

Words he would use, his humour, warmth, the kind

Of life he led, the splendour he would find

In ordinary things of everyday,

The richness of his thought, the interplay

Of wit and learning, casually combined.


But Christ!  I'm speaking as though he were dead!

By God!  He's far from that.  Likely he's out

On the booze with a crowd of friends, or settling down

With his latest bird by now, whilst I, instead,

Skulk here at home, with his book and read about

His life.  I know he'd rather I hit the town!

*1980*

# Poets' Testament

A cow without its plaid,

A plough that lacks its coat,

Might well become afraid

Of tram lines, or a boat.

Believe the subtle sage

The faithful poet trust,

A piece of fish will age,

And ink is only dust.

The time is nearly come

When rose leaves grow in size -

Some shrivel up, while some

Make garnishing for pies.

So leave the well - lit street,

Steer from the lighted walk,

Betake your pensive feet

To where the poets talk.

*1997*

## Rondel (after Villon)

Every dolly bird and boy,

When they feel the touch of spring

Hit the trail and shout and sing,

Do their thing and shout for joy,

Burn the road up, and annoy

Everyone and everything -

Every dolly bird and boy -

When they feel the touch of spring.

Off they go (the hoi polloi!)

Dig their speed, their gambolling!

How they love the ding a ding!

(Dressed in jeans or corduroy) -

Every dolly bird and boy.

*1969*

# Unicorn

The unicorn that lies in Mary's lap
Is pierced by a sharp sword inlaid with gold,
Around the wound the blood flows drop by drop
As on her breast it lays its lovely head.

The milk - white unicorn that Mary loves
Is riven by a silver pointed spear
But in its eyes there dwells a holy peace
Over its cheek there strays its golden hair.

There stands one with an iron - headed axe;
Its burnished edge is fringed with drying blood;
But sweetest pity in the virgin's looks
Watches the mingling of the white and red.

Is there salve to close the staring wounds?
Is there balm to soothe the searing pain?
Or have they hold upon those slender strands?
To twist his life stem like his twisted horn?

*from 'Wartime Harvest', ed. Geoffrey Treece, Bale & Staples 1943*

# Loving

# LOVING

# An Offering For Jane's Birthday

Jewels? - she rejects them, posts them back again!

Amethysts, rubies, onyxes or pearls -

None she accepts; treats them with disdain -

Everyone says she's not like other girls -

And never fails to make her meaning plain:

No presents (and no flowers) for Miss Jane!

Do not give nylon.  Send her mink in vain.

Even exquisite perfumes she'll return.

Remember - if her friendship you'd retain -

Send no rare volumes: these she'll surely burn.

Observe this rule (or you'll cause her pain).

No presents and no flowers for Miss Jane!

*1958*

# How Her Hair Fell

waves
of the sea
fell sheer

so her hair
glittering shines and falls

waves of her hair
shimmer and fall
away and fall

fall swaying

glitter
fall
and shine

shimmer
sway
and fall

waves
of the sea
fall sheer

so her hair
glittering shines
and falls

*1968*

# My Darling Beside Me

My darling beside me singing

Our feet on the road up the hill

The great yellow moon through the black branches

High above a star with many rays

A ghostly cross at the centre

Roaring from the cross

To shatter its bright prison

Or split the sky

Up from our own tiny cone of happiness

Our eyes the centre of the circle of the sky

The same journey every way to infinity

The centre at peace

Men in the sky.

*undated*

# Ultimate Love Poem

Some call you virtuous, others call you whore:

You walk into a room and I adore.

I love whatever love permits.

I love your cunt; I love your tits.

I love you everywhere.

I love your smudge of pubic hair,

Your arse, your nose, down on your face.

I love your every secret place.

I love you sober, love you pissed,

Intimate, cool, coquettish, kissed.

Love you awake or sleeping.  Love you mad.

Love you angelic, childlike.  Love you bad.

Love you destructive, crazy, wild and weird,

Caring and kindly, wild and feared.

Love you stripped and love you dressed.

Love you ecstatic.  Love you distressed.

I love your ears.  I love your tongue.

I love you timid, love you bold.

I love you wholly now you're young.

I'll love you when you're old.

*1996*

18

# Laughing

# LAUGHING

# Tall Girl

TALL
girl
tall as me
MUST be
a TALL GIRL
to be
as tall as ME

not just a girl
not JUST a girl
but a
tall
tall
girl
as tall as me

as TALL as ME
a girl
NOT just a GIRL
but a GIRL as TALL as ME

so TALL
tall tall tall girl
GIRL
just about my height
a TALL girl

*1967*

# The Brothers Blake

The brothers Blake were gaily brave
While they were walking near the grave.
When Robert's spirit broke the bands
Tied by the flesh it clapped his hands,
And William, dying, raised his strong
Melodious voice in tuneful song.

*1949*

# The Height Of Fashion

A lady called Pavlova Higgs

Was addicted to Pompadour wigs.

They were piled up so high

That they reached to the sky

And brought down a couple of MIGs.

*1996*

# The Question

WHO?

## WHODIDYOUSAY?

who

## WHO?

WHO


WHo

Who

who


who-o-o-o
Who-o-o-o?



# WHO

## WHo

Who

who

wh

w


*1968*

# Terry's War

# TERRY'S WAR

# First Attack

in colchester bands played

the clockwork bandmaster raised

his stave in a white hand

the tanks galloped across the sand

the first shot flays

the membrane of a big drum

and as the dive bombers came

a huge crowd cried

a great laugh leapt

from a hotel window

where a girl lolls

her cigarette falls

a gay waterfall of blood

on a stiff khaki tunic

ahead of the tanks bandsmen die

trumpet and fife crushed

the bandmaster flickered his stick

strutted in glossy shoes

mud grasped his feet

a bomb split the street

stifling people's shout

limbs silently dragged

into the shattering darkness pegged

heads to the red sky

*undated*

# I Lost My Way

I lost my way among some strange machines;

I had been guided through the metal lanes

By broken memories of departed days

Then found I did not know which way to choose

Because within the tangled, clanging mass

I saw nothing I knew.

I jerked my head from side to side

In terror.

My eyes tried to pierce the rising gloom.

I turned and fled.

*undated*

# From The Tall Walls

From the tall walls of the grey town

The sweet dissolute faces of the painted

Girls smiling from dizzy casements wept

Into our eager hands.  Red fire

Dripped from their finger nails.

Probed our young limbs.

A gun

Of glass protruded from the giant's mouth.

Trees grew bravely in his hair.  His face was ploughed

With steel. Long snakes

Writhed, knotted in his stomach.

No bank clerk, nor dustman

(Gaily jesting hero), nor postman,

Nor undertaker, nor city tart

Nor country lout, nor mechanic,

Nor plumber's mate, nor rag picker,

Nor bishop, nor journalist, nor pigeon fancier,

Nor bricklayer, nor Member of Parliament

Nor any of the thousand and one stuck - up

Little runts any suburb spawns,

Could help him, poor fool.


So we advanced upon his limbs, and crushed

The flesh.  The face was split.

His skull broken and the brains oozed out

Like lava, turning into butterflies,

A blue, red, green, yellow

Delicate ballet of fairy whisps.

*undated*

# Recruit

My body in its rough serge remembered too well

The scholar's gown.  My hands found hard exchange

For the easy pen; but these were small things.

I came a stranger among them, innocent,

Blushing at their rich oaths and animal ways.

I had no armour for my sensitive heart.

I flinched at every loud word as at a blow.

I walked in a misty cloud of vanishing

Illusion suddenly pierced at every turn

By their bright shafts of unconsidered utterance.

Their laughter clattered into the peaceful rooms

Of my quiet mind trailing a wreckage of shattered thought.

That was not all.

To them, I thought, I must

Appear a meek intruder, a fit object for

Offhand, summary criticism and ribald comment.

I groped gently in this wild forest

For a gateway into the unknown realms of other minds.

The gateway was in my own soul.

My fineclothed intellect

Bowed in humility before the high pride

Of nude power and I was free to love.

# Infantryman

Now the time has come for the heavy artillery

Loud - voiced,  and to swing high over my head,

Fierce herald of the attack, ribbing the sky.

The planes above are creeping over the earth's ceiling.

Light feels towards the grey, unknown antagonist.

Now the mountainous iron tanks, inhuman, unfeeling

Throb with the surge of their powerful, harsh - tongued

engines,

Grind forward, splintering stones with their steel feet.

Now is the time to slide back the silver bolt

And press the austere round up the rifle's spout,

To run a sensitive finger along the cool bayonet,

To ease the web straps straining the shoulder blades,

To crush the last cigarette under the boot heel.

For we are near the end of the journey

And the setting down of burdens.

Like children from school we shall burst

Into this playground, and the choice

Of two freedoms shall be decided for us.

*1939 - 1945*

# Good Friday 1942

Last night there was a heavy raid

And today rumours run from mouth to mouth.

Who knows who caught the too elusive truth?

Tonight the men talk of their own things,

Of their homes, hopes, longings.

One lived on a farm and was happy;

Another smiles, talking of the girl he hopes to marry;

'I was taught skill with my hands',

Says one, 'And it shall serve me when this war ends.'

These things are shadows, tricks of fate,

Reality, the state of things which wait.

There is no panic nor a hint of fear

In the eyes of these men waiting here.

In their eyes their lives no hate,

For they muse on their own things,

Each man apart.

*undated*

# Tank Talk

The tanks are talking.  'It is strange',
Said one, 'that those who ride within
Bring us so closely into range
Of those who are our hostile kin.'

'Why should this be?  Why cannot they
Sit in their fields as we do now?'
Another stirred and answered, 'Nay,
Such peace the riders won't allow.'

'What is this talk?', a third one said.
'What are these things we have to do?'
An old one slowly raised its head
And said, 'You know not.  You are new.'

A dented thing beside him spoke:
'They set these tasks that we may feel
Our power in the noise and smoke
And know the hardness of our steel.'

'But, friend,' said one.  'I call to mind

Times when the hard steel has been split.

I have seen brothers left behind -

And much have I regretted it.'


'Indeed,' the first agreed, 'I too

Have seen such sights as you recall.'

One murmured, 'It's the riders who

Decide the pattern of it all.'


He added, 'and the riders must

Run dangers in the fierce exchange,

For they have no hard metal crust

But fragile stuff called flesh...It's strange...'


*1945*

# Tunisia 1943

Hair was gold lamb's wool, curly crisp,

Crisp in spring, a youth's crown.

Hands were lithe to petal the wheel of a car.

Legs were tender firm on accelerator and clutch

To skim the swift machine on the tender road rim

Of a great city.  Tall towers of stone

Were home, echoing with brave laughter.


Now he is broken: a china doll flung from a child's hands

White limbs blood laced, shattered.


He gave his blood to cement a fair city

That what he knew might be known by those he knew not.

Neither knew he this.  Unknowing, in love of life

He embraced death gladly.

*1943*

# France 1944

The corn was ripening and the apples swelled

On the rich trees.  The friendly French bestowed

Choice gifts of plums and peaches on us as

We passed their cottages in strange machines.

They were so ready to forgive the charred

And tortured villages we left behind.

For our advance was slowly purging all

The insidious terror that had crept into

Their homes to choke their hearts and film their eyes.

And in those dangerous and heroic days

We never knew, being preoccupied,

What an immense adventure we began.

We little dreamed, as we lay folded deep

In Norman lanes, of the long vistas that

Extended into distant battle fields.

Suddenly, riveted on to the earth

By a swift shell's just audible approach,

We had no time to ponder history,

No thought to strike a liberator's pose.

No heart for drama or for high design.

There was but time to visualise a face

Seen through familiar windows, or a hand

That blossomed in farewell from some grey platform.

*1944*

# Tank Attack

The cloud of dust we trailed intimated our approach;

From mother war's womb we re-emerged resplendent

In panoply of armour plate our machines

Yelling like lusty children lurching towards life

On ungainly feet.  The morning laughed

At our pretension with Spring brazenness.

As we forged our plans for the rapid factory

Of minds trained on decisions we apprehended.

The white horizon and the grey outline of the forest.

We held ourselves erect, taut, expectant.

Life sprang forth with the first shot.

Our intellect's Hamlet, pricked into action

Found manhood's pride in swift bodily motion.

The sun rose high overhead cheering

Like a summer's day.  The machines blossomed.

Stored - up energy released its hoarded power.

This was the supreme moment of war's embrace.

Battle.

When it had concluded its final, uneven convulsions

And after we had lain for a moment at peace

Those who were able, crept forward into the new positions.

At nightfall we heard that the operation had been successful

And said farewell to the dead as we left amid the destruction.

The bodies entered prematurely into the heritage

Of old age.  Their promise drowned like Prospero's books.

*undated*

# Farm House

Penetrating beyond the beaches,

Seeking ease for my heart,

In conflict of the body,

I saw a shelled farmhouse burning,

Blazing calmly to its own peace

To relief from all stresses.

From stress of time on timber,

Of timber on brick, to rest from its labour.

It lolled, a black skeleton in a green hollow.

Passing it by and moving towards the horizon,

I saw the skeleton become a jewel of blood

Ready to thread on my string of beads.

*undated*

# Tunisian Advance

between the scrub and the sky

between terror and love

they came down the valley

one by one, rising from cover


the giant in the sky

watched them creeping

hardly heard gun fire

saw a few of them dropping


the sky filled a man's eyes

as he lay in peace

with the sorrow of sunset

across his quiet face


the other brown shadows

went forward ceaselessly

to meet a dark lover

under the night sky

*undated*

# Advance Into Germany

And there were some who left the centre - line

To stray into the green and treacherous fields.

These were the ones we hardly knew were gone,

Whose names we heard while lying half asleep

In shattered rooms, and very quietly said,

'I thought I hadn't seen him for a while.

I never knew that they had got him too.'

And some of these had waited day by day,

Knowing that they were doomed, whom jagged steel

Welcomed as brothers.  Others had been fierce

In their demand on life, to whom there was

No meaning but in sense and action, whose

Demise took them all unawares and as

They lay in silence and in stillness.  From

Their eyes stared a frozen question: Why?

And some lie sheltering now, dug deep into

Convenient earthworks, as though waiting for

A new and sudden order to advance.

Such friends we lost.  And yet we always found

Fresh comrades for the adventure, but we felt

The ache of half - healed scars upon our hearts

That little tricks of memory made raw.

*1945*

# Special Mission

Where the drapery of delicate branches

Was green lace

He smiled at the light caresses

Touching his face.


A bird on a bushy twist,

A ragged throne,

Cries farewell from the forest;

And he was alone.


He entered the open grassland,

A lonely invader,

Impertinent to try to understand

The plan of his leader.


The machine guns jabbered

And artillery slammed

Like the door of an empty cupboard,

Loneliness was shamed.

Above brooded the dark bombers.
He, on his knees, a child
In a woolly suit, remembers
Crawling towards the trees.

The pilot banked his machine
Peering through the glass
At the smudge, motionless and brown,
Ungainly, on the grass.

*undated*

# For KPT Twenty One Years Old

Poetry's thankless work in this dull age

Which damns alike the poet and the sage:

When interest, pride and avarice accuse,

Few have the courage to defend the muse.

But virtue of the subject shall defend

These lines in commendation of a friend,

And blunt the taunts of those who would decry

The power and place of living poetry.


Beneath the white rose was the birth

    When April with his showers sweet

Watered the newly seeded earth

    And fields were soft beneath the feet.


The nest was fine, the birds were fair,

    And brave the murmuring of doves,

But there was influence in the air

    Foreign to ordinary loves.

For something strange was to be born

    But no one knew that from this nest

  Would rise (no comet there to warn)

    A bird of colour and unrest.


It rose with fledgling plumes of many eyes.

    Its voice, though young, was harsh and strange.

  It rose - the colours dimmed the morning skies.

    It rose.  Its voice increased in power and range.

It seemed a beauty as of brightest day;

The golden ball of heaven's eternal fire

That danced with glory on the silver waves

One moment hid his head in jealous shame,

Thinking the bird was some new - risen sun

That trailed its glory on the firmament.

Then, though no mortal saw the strange event

The angels walked upon the walls of heaven

As sentinels to warn the immortal souls

That an outrageous bird had come on earth

    Jealousy from sun -

        Jeopardy from angels.

*1948*

# War Poem

A WORD
WAR
A WORD

WAR

war
war
WAR

AWARE?

war
war
WAR

WAR
WAR
WAR

war
a word
a word

*1967*

# LIST OF POEMS

www.ingramcontent.com/pod-product-compliance
Lightning Source LLC
Chambersburg PA
CBHW041431040426
42445CB00020B/1981